Own your Period

by Chella Quint

Illustrated by Giovana Medeiros

To Leona and Gaetano. This book is *eventually* for you! And to my family, friends, and supporters of Period Positive. Thank you for helping me want this book to happen. — *C.Q.*

To Angelica and Talita, who have always helped to guide me—not only through my teen years but into adulthood too. — *G.M.*

Quarto is the authority on a wide range of topics.

Quarto educates, entertains and enriches the lives of our readers—enthusiasts and lovers of hands-on living.

www.quartoknows.com

Designer: Sarah Chapman-Suire
Commissioning Editor: Carly Madden
Creative Director: Malena Stojic
Associate Publisher: Holly Willsher
Project Manager: Nancy Dickmann
Consultant: Dr. Charlotte Elder

First published in 2021 by QEB Publishing, an imprint of The Quarto Group.
26391 Crown Valley Parkway, Suite 220, Mission Viejo, CA 92691, USA.
T: +1 949 380 7510 F: +1 949 380 7575
www.QuartoKnows.com

A CIP record for this book is available from the Library of Congress.

The publishers and author cannot be held responsible for the content of the apps and websites referred to in this book. All web addresses were correct at the time of printing.

ISBN 978 0 7112 5664 4
Manufactured in Guangdong, China TT052021
9 8 7 6 5 4 3 2 1

The author would like to gratefully acknowledge: Giovana Medeiros for bringing my ideas, my work, and my life... to life, and the entire team at Quarto Kids and everyone else who had a hand in creating this book, for making this experience even lovelier than I ever could have imagined. Thank you.

Contents

Hello from Chella!

When I was younger, I was anxious about the changes I heard were going to happen to me as I grew up. I had a lot of questions, but periods seemed like something people avoided talking about. I didn't want anyone else to be worried about this subject, so I went to college and studied periods! I learned that getting all the facts and having fun helped people feel more confident about menstruation. This let them talk openly, complain if they wanted to, ask questions confidently, and share what they knew with others. I decided to describe this attitude as being **period positive!**

This book will tell you all about what to expect, how it works, and what it can feel like. You'll also learn how to challenge negative attitudes about periods. Even if you don't need to know all of these facts right now, you can always come back and reread parts of this book as you get older. **Own Your Period** will be right here when you need it.

Chella X

5

who is this book for?

This book is mostly for anyone who is probably about to get their first period or who has recently started. That's why I am mostly talking to **"you"** throughout the book. So if **"you"** means *you*, congratulations! Having your period is a pretty amazing thing that your body can do, and it's great to know all about it. After all, it's *your* period and it belongs to you!

But I'm not someone who gets periods. Can I still read this book?

Of course! This book may be directed at period owners, but if you don't get periods, you don't have to stop reading! Periods are interesting, and it's important to learn about other people's experiences, even if they don't affect you directly. That way you'll be able to support your friends and family and community and help make it fairer. Anyway, everyone grew inside a uterus once. So even if you don't have one, you used to live inside one—and you're right to be interested in how one works!

So who does get periods then?

Most people who have periods get their first one between the ages of 9 and 16, but the average age is about 12-and-a-bit years old. A few start a couple of years earlier, at about 7 or 8 years old. This is a little unusual, but it's certainly not impossible. Some people who get periods do not identify as girls, and may be non-binary, gender fluid, trans guys, or intersex. And some girls or women whom you may expect to have them may not ever get periods at all. This might be because of how their bodies developed before they were born, or because they had a serious illness.

No matter what, though, if you are someone who already has periods, or you're going to start soon, or you want to find out more about what periods might be like for your friends or siblings now and as you get older, then this book is for you!

7

THE BASICS

When I was studying periods, I talked to a lot of kids about the best way to teach it, and they said not to leave anything out. So I haven't! Talking about periods means using some words that may not be familiar to you. Knowing a bit of science background will also help you understand how your body works. This section explains these words and facts, because some of them will come up a lot as you read the rest of this book. You may know some of these things already. If so, that's great! If not, don't worry! You'll be an expert before you know it.

periods and puberty

Periods are part of puberty ... and puberty is a part of growing up. Puberty is the name we give to the time when children's bodies start to grow into adult bodies. When you first hear about it, puberty may seem like a really big change that will happen all at once, but it is actually much more gradual.

Think about it this way: most of the things that your body does started when you were a baby. When you were born, you could already sleep and eat and pee and poop and cry. Before long you learned to smile and laugh, and then to move around and communicate some more.

But all of those changes happened slowly, probably without you noticing, until maybe you outgrew your shoes or could reach a light switch for the first time. You have been learning new skills and words and getting bigger all this time. Puberty may be the part of growing up that we happen to have a name for, but you've been growing and changing your whole life—and you are already very good at it!

What's your story?

You might not remember your earliest growing-up milestones, such as getting your first tooth, or starting school. Can you remember losing your first baby tooth? If you don't, someone in your family probably will! There may be a photo of you with missing front teeth, or someone may have written down the details.

Menstru-what?

You may have already heard of periods from your friends or a relative or a teacher. You also may have heard the word "menstruation." They both mean the same thing—menstruation is the actual word, while period is a nickname. It is short for "menstrual period." You will see the words "menstruation," "menstrual," and "period" a lot in this book.

Not everyone feels comfortable talking about menstruation, so a lot of people try to avoid the topic. Can you remember the first time you heard about periods or menstruation? What was the mood or attitude at the time? Ask your friends—they may have had a similar experience.

menstruation menstruáció MENSTRUATIE
менструация menstruatsioon
MENSTRACIJOS
ENSTRUACIJOS
MISLIF
estruazzjoni
miesiączka
enštruácia
menštruácijas
IOSTRÚ
menstruació
IMÁSINA
menstruasjon
menstruacija
MENSTRUACE
menstruação mestruazione
MENSTRUCIJO MENSTRUACIÓN
менструацнja

What's a vulva?

You may already know that during a period, blood comes out of the vagina, which opens into a part of the body called the vulva. The vulva is at the front of the pelvis, where the legs join, and it is the name for the parts of the reproductive system that are on the outside of the body. This bleeding is not an injury or an illness—it's a regular thing that bodies do.

What does a vulva look like?

People come in lots of different shapes and sizes, with different skin tones and hairstyles ... and so do vulvas! If you look between your legs in a full-length mirror, you will see your own vulva. You can't see your vulva just by looking down from above, but if you sit down and hold up a smaller mirror you can see more detail. You can even use a flashlight.

A vulva can look like this ... or this ... or this ...

On the outside

There is often pubic hair on the outside of the vulva. This hair starts growing during puberty and can cover a small, medium, or large area of the vulva. It can also cover parts of the thighs, belly, and bottom. It usually covers the mons pubis, which is a mound at the top of the vulva that grows thicker at the start of puberty.

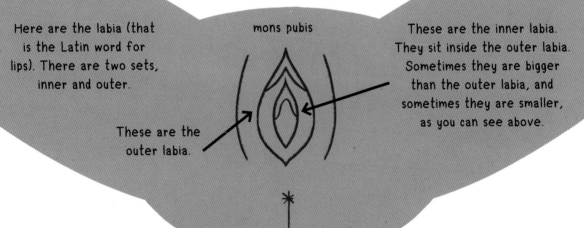

Here are the labia (that is the Latin word for lips). There are two sets, inner and outer.

mons pubis

These are the inner labia. They sit inside the outer labia. Sometimes they are bigger than the outer labia, and sometimes they are smaller, as you can see above.

These are the outer labia.

Different is good!

Each person is different, and so is the shape of their labia. Some are bigger, some are smaller. Some are thicker, some are thinner. Some hang down a bit or are wide apart, and some are tucked in and close together. Some labia are the same size and shape on both sides and some are different. Some are darker or lighter than most of the rest of someone's skin tone. Some labia have a bit of hair, others have a lot and some will grow hair one day. The hair can be curly, or wavy, or straight. Some vulvas are wrinkly and some are smooth. Some have a mole or freckles, and some do not. Everyone is different! Even the way your own vulva looks will change as you go through puberty.

THE BASICS

Parts of the vulva

The area inside the inner labia is a little harder to see, but it is still part of the vulva. It has many different parts.

The urethral opening leads to the urethra —the tube that takes your pee from your bladder to the outside of your body.

The Skene's glands (also called paraurethral glands) produce lubrication for the urethra.

This opening is the vaginal opening—the entrance to your vagina. Menstrual blood comes out of your vagina.

The greater vestibular glands (also called Bartholin's glands) are on the inner labia. These produce lubrication for the vagina.

The perineum is the area between the vulva and the anus. It is very sensitive because of a sensitive, spongy area just below the surface.

Inside your labia, at the top, is the hood of the clitoris. Some people can see the hood when they look at their vulva, while on other vulvas it is more tucked in.

The hood covers a very sensitive part of the clitoris called the glans. The glans may be too sensitive to touch, but the hood protects it. Many people enjoy touching the different parts of their clitoris in order to have an orgasm.

You can't see the rest of the clitoris from the outside. It is just under the surface, surrounded by sensitive skin and strong muscle. It reaches all along your labia. It is very sensitive when touched, and you might feel the sensations all around the outside of the vulva, vaginal opening, and down toward your perineum.

The fourchette is a very thin bit of skin that joins the labia together. "Fourchette" is the French word for "fork," and this part is like a fork in the road where your labial skin divides into two pathways.

The anus is the opening where poop leaves the rectum. It is below the perineum.

Some people call their vulva their vagina, but this is actually incorrect. The vulva is all of the body parts covered on pages 12-15, which are on the *outside* of your body. The vaginal *opening* can be seen if you examine your vulva, but you cannot see your vagina from outside the body. Why not look in a mirror and try drawing your vulva?

THE BASICS

Inside your body

Your vulva connects to the rest
reproductive system, but these
on the *inside*—you can't see the
a mirror! Here is a drawing that
what they look like.

The oviducts lead to the uterus, or womb. They enter just below the top of the uterus.

The two ovaries are where
cells grow. Egg cells are some
called by their Latin name, ov
one is called an ovum).

A mature egg cell travels down an oviduct, often called a Fallopian tube.

The endometrium is the lining of the uterus.

(This drawing isn't to scale. Ovaries are about the size of almonds and your uterus is about the size of your fist!)

The cervix is the ring of muscular tissue that forms the neck of the uterus. It opens into the vagina. The entrance to the cervix can open and close during ovulation, menstruation, and childbirth. It can be high or low, and can be tipped forward or backward.

The cervix leads to the vagina, which is a muscular organ that can expand and contract. The vaginal opening leads out of your body as part of your vulva.

If you like, push a finger into your vagina to gently try to feel your cervix. If your fingers are long enough (and your cervix is low enough), you will just about touch something that feels like a little donut. That's your cervix!

My story

When I was studying periods, I learned that Fallopian tubes, Bartholin's glands, and Skene's glands were named after the doctors who first wrote articles about those body parts. It made me feel a bit like these doctors thought those body parts were *theirs*, not mine. And none of these doctors ever even had a period! Back then it was very difficult to go to college (or medical school) if you were someone who had periods. So I've shared alternative names which explain what that part does or where it is. A lot of people writing about periods are starting to do this, and it is a great way to work toward owning your period.

Periods and hormones

Did you know that our brains and bodies run on chemistry? Chemicals called hormones help our organs work—including the organs that control the menstrual cycle. We couldn't get by without hormones! They are produced by organs called endocrine glands, which make up the endocrine system.

Puberty and hormones

Hormones cause the visible changes in your body that happen during puberty, such as getting taller or growing back molar teeth. Hormones also tell your reproductive organs to grow to their adult size. The steps are led by a variety of different hormones, and the timing and age you are varies. Here are the glands and hormones that help make periods possible. (Some hormones have very long names and go by their initials.)

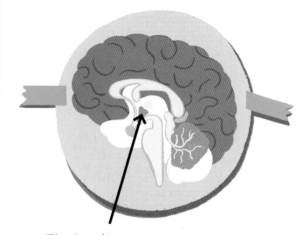

The hypothalamus is inside your brain. It makes a hormone called GnRH that sends a message to your pituitary gland, telling it to release other hormones, FSH and LH.

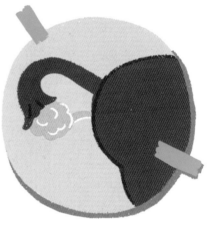

The ovaries produce estrogen. Estrogen and another hormone called progesterone work together to tell the cervix which kind of mucus to produce at different times in the menstrual cycle. Estrogen also helps egg cells develop until they are mature enough to leave the follicle, and it helps the endometrium to get thicker too. Each used egg follicle then changes jobs and begins to produce progesterone.

The pituitary gland is in your brain. It's small, but very important! It produces FSH, which tells the follicles in your ovaries to start to grow and prepare to release eggs. The pituitary gland also makes LH, which helps an egg to grow and be released from the ovary.

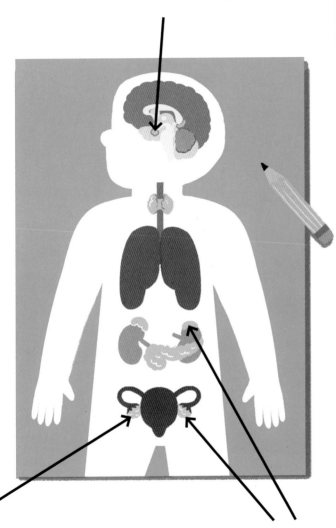

Working together

The endocrine system is just one of your body's systems. You also have a digestive system, circulatory system, respiratory system, and more. We call these "systems" because each one is a collection of different organs, fluids, and chemicals that work together to get each job done. They are like the parts of a very cool, organic, squishy machine!

When levels of progesterone drop, that tells the uterus to shed its lining. Progesterone is mainly produced in the ovaries, but it is also made by the adrenal glands—one above each kidney. The ovaries and adrenal glands also produce small amounts of testosterone. This hormone influences energy, arousal, muscles, and mood.

THE BASICS

Menstrual cycle phases

For people who get periods, the reproductive system involves four steps, which happen in a cycle. Paying attention to each of the stages of menstruation as they happen in your body—and noticing how you feel—is a great way to focus on your health and wellbeing. Doing the things that make you feel your best at each stage can easily become a very healthy and useful habit!

Phase 1: the period

A period actually comes at the end of the whole process, but it's the easiest sign to spot (no pun intended!), so we count each new cycle from the first day of the period. During this phase, your uterus cramps or squeezes to help you physically drain away blood and tissue. You can also feel very emotionally drained. You might feel tired or slow, and early in your period you might feel a deep heaviness in your body. Cramps can feel worse on the first couple of days of your period.

During this phase, you may feel like hibernating or re-watching your favorite TV shows. You may find you feel better after doing a relaxing activity, and that you feel worse if you have a very busy schedule. On the other hand, some people prefer to stay active and busy during this phase!

Phase 2: the follicular phase

This phase varies in length, and it's usually the reason that one person's cycle might be a different length than another person's. While you are in this phase, your body is thinking about being productive and creative—it's literally maturing an egg! The sensation can work emotionally too. This point in your cycle is a great time to try out a new creative project, sport, or activity, or to hang out with new friends for the first time. Why not experiment for a few months and try to do new stuff while you're growing a new egg? Just remember: not everyone notices this to be true about their bodies. So don't worry if it doesn't seem to work for you!

Phase 3: ovulation

This is the phase of the menstrual cycle when some people find they have the most energy. Some find it helpful to try new things here, but others feel too excited and want to just be social and have fun. You may feel excited or aroused more easily, or even find people you like are more attractive. While you're ovulating, or just after, you may even find it easier to do homework you've been putting off. Your mood may help you tackle anything that takes a lot of stamina and determination.

My story

It took me a long time to recognize this behavior in myself, even though I was studying periods! Sometimes I would feel argumentative, or like everyone was out to get me, and would go to bed angry. Then I would wake up the next morning and realize sheepishly that I had just started my period. It took me way too long to notice that I'd been very grumpy about something unimportant AGAIN, on the exact same day of my cycle. Every month.

Phase 4: the luteal phase

This phase is usually about the same length of time for everyone—about 14 days. However, if you ovulate earlier in your cycle than most people, you may feel like it lasts a loooooong time. It's easy to go from feeling creative to feeling cranky. You may feel paranoid or like nobody likes you. It can feel really yucky and you may have to work hard to convince yourself that it's your hormones that are making you jumpy.

Try to remind yourself that little things are no big deal, and take a break or a time out if you feel like you're going to lose your temper. If you wait a day or two, you may realize that you were about to get very angry about something that isn't as big a deal as you thought.

23

BABY

Life cycle of a period

You grow and change throughout your life. And your periods change too! As you get older, you will go through different stages. Everyone who gets periods will go through the same stages, but usually at slightly different times.

Pre-puberty

This may really surprise you, but the timeline of your period starts two generations before you! When you were born, your ovaries were already formed. The same thing goes for your mother. This means that while *she* was developing in *her* mother's uterus, she had egg cells inside her ovaries. One of these egg cells matured and was fertilized and grew up to be *you*. So a tiny part of you was in your grandmother's uterus!

You were born with about 2 million egg cells in your ovaries, and a tiny uterus of your own. As a toddler and young child you were growing and developing in lots of other ways inside and out, but your uterus, ovaries, vagina, and vulva were still not mature.

Puberty

During puberty, your glands send out hormones and your reproductive organs start maturing. You start to develop in more visible ways too. You get taller, your hips may become rounder and your breasts grow. The size and shape your body grows into is something you mostly inherit, and is usually similar to how other relatives looked at that age.

24

Menarche

Menarche is the word for the time when you get your first period. Your periods begin at this point, but they probably won't happen regularly at first.

Late teens/early twenties

Your brain continues developing and maturing, even after your body's growth has mostly slowed down. It starts making connections that help you make decisions more logically and thoughtfully, and you become more aware of your emotions and values. The hormones that control your periods usually settle into a pattern. Even though you were fertile just before your periods started, you may be only just starting to make decisions about preventing pregnancy. You may start becoming clearer about the qualities you find attractive in others and about what makes you feel good.

Fertile years

In your twenties and thirties you may be making decisions about whether you want to become pregnant or not. You may choose to start a family. Some people find that while pregnant they are a bit forgetful or feel like their thoughts are a bit foggy, but this goes away. Periods usually stop during pregnancy, and often during breastfeeding too. After giving birth, the change in hormones may affect your mental health for a time. This can be difficult, but support is available. By your late thirties to early forties it may become harder to get pregnant, but it is still possible and many people do.

Perimenopause begins

In your mid to late forties you may notice that your periods or cycles become shorter, or you may see spots of blood at the start of each cycle. You may not have ovulated before each period. This is a gradual process, so you may not notice it happening. It is very difficult to become pregnant without fertility help at this stage, though some people do. Hormone tests may show lower levels of egg reserves and that you are producing fewer reproductive hormones. Later in this phase, periods can be irregular—almost like back when you first started menstruating.

Sometimes cycles are heavier or last for more days than usual, and sometimes periods are lighter or even absent. This is because perimenopause involves a big change in hormone levels, which has many effects on different body systems. These effects can start before your very last period, and continue for a few months or years after it. You may experience dry skin, a dry mouth and less lubrication in your vagina. You could find it harder to fall asleep and you may feel too warm sometimes. You can also feel a bit foggy in your thoughts from time to time, or be forgetful, just like during pregnancy, but this also goes away. Some people choose to take hormones that make this transition smoother by allowing the hormone levels to change more gradually through menopause and beyond.

Menopause

Menopause is the word for the end of having menstrual cycles. Many doctors agree that if you can look back at your cycle chart and see that you haven't had periods for a year, you have reached menopause.

Post-menopause

From around your late fifties onward, you no longer ovulate or have periods. As you produce fewer hormones, you may notice your hair gradually thin, and your weight may shift so you have a thicker core. You should find that you feel much more alert, active, and creative than you did during your menopause transition. It's time to enjoy the next stage of your life.

Having babies?!?

Once you start puberty, your ovaries start producing mature egg cells. If one of these combines with a sperm cell from someone else and implants in the uterus, it could lead to pregnancy.

When I first heard that as a kid, I was like... hang on, I'm not ready to have babies! And I was right! Our *bodies* may mature quickly, but our emotions mature much more slowly. The way that a brain learns to process our feelings, make decisions and form healthy relationships takes a *lot* longer—into your twenties, in fact. As people grow up, some may decide they don't want to have children at all. Others decide they don't want to become pregnant before they are ready to start a family, and may use some form of contraception.

Getting pregnant

If an adult does decide to become pregnant, there are a lot of ways it can happen. People in relationships where one person produces healthy eggs and another person produces healthy sperm may be able to start a pregnancy pretty easily. Did you know that it's not always possible to become pregnant, even if someone wants to? They may be in a relationship with someone who cannot produce sperm. They may have gone through menopause or have a medical issue that makes it difficult to get or stay pregnant. This is called subfertility or infertility.

Fertility support

Luckily, there are many types of fertility support. A person can take hormones to help them ovulate. Sperm can be inserted into the uterus, through the cervix, to give them a better chance of fertilizing the egg. They can also be inserted into an egg in a lab and then implanted into the uterus—this is called IVF. Some families have help from a sperm donor, egg donor, or surrogate person who will carry the baby in their uterus. Some families choose to donate their eggs, sperm, or embryos, or become surrogates for others.

These treatments don't always work, may not be available, or can take a long time. It is important to know about all of this long before you decide about having children or not. Luckily, you don't have to make any decisions for a long time!

Starting a family

When and if you do feel ready to start a family, there are a lot of ways to do it. Only some of them involve you being someone who has periods or being in a relationship with someone who produces sperm. Some people parent a partner's children from a previous relationship. Others adopt children or become foster parents. Some people wish to become a parent alone. Some people help raise their younger siblings or nieces and nephews. It's pretty great that there are so many different kinds of family!

29

Period stats

Did you ever wonder how much blood comes out during a period? Or how long people have periods for? Luckily, there is now a lot of data available about menstrual cycles. It comes from doctors and researchers asking large numbers of people about their periods, over many years.

Everyone is different, so menstrual stats are usually discussed as an average. It's absolutely fine if your numbers are different from that average. It's more helpful to think about whether your personal stats fall within a range of healthy numbers. What you're experiencing is probably similar to what's happening for other people. You can find out by asking! Your friends or relatives might share their stats with you. If you have biological relatives with periods, ask them when they started and what their flow is like, to get an idea of how yours might be.

What if I'm off the chart?

Some periods don't fit within the range. You may start late or stop early, or have a heavier or lighter flow, or a longer or shorter cycle. Sometimes there is a medical reason for it, like a change in hormones or diet, stress, or illness. If your cycle is out of a lot of the ranges here, or if it suddenly changes in some way, you can talk to your doctor.

Age at menarche:
9-16 years old

Length of cycle for adults:
21-35 days

Length of cycle for
young people: 21-45 days

Number of menstrual cycles
per year: 11-13

Length of period:
less than 7 days

Days until ovulation
Young people: 7-31 days
Adults: 7-21 days

Amount of blood each cycle:
2-6 tablespoons

Number of eggs in the
ovaries at birth: 1-2 million

Number of eggs left at
puberty: 300,000

Number of eggs ovulated by
one person over a lifetime:
400-500

Number of years people
have periods:
about 40 years

Age at menopause:
45-55 years old

My story

I started my period when I was 12½ and
my mom did when she was 11. But her mom,
who emigrated from another country to
escape danger, didn't start until she was 17.
This kind of stress can delay menarche.

MANAGING PERIODS

People used to use phrases like "coping with periods" or "dealing with periods." These words made it seem like menstruation was unwanted or bad, which made some folks feel embarrassed about having periods. That's why I think of it as "managing," because when you manage something, it means you're taking care of it.

When you take good care of yourself, you're being kind and looking after your emotions and your body. Taking care can also mean being responsible for something in a practical way. When you manage periods, you're doing both. Making decisions about managing your body and your health helps you feel proud and confident.

what do periods look like?

Menstrual blood looks different for different people at different times of their cycle and at different times in their lives. And it's not just blood! What comes out of your body is actually the thickened lining of the endometrium—the inside wall of the uterus. It is normally made up of blood cells and tissue cells from the endometrium wall itself, as well as mucus and fluid produced by the vagina.

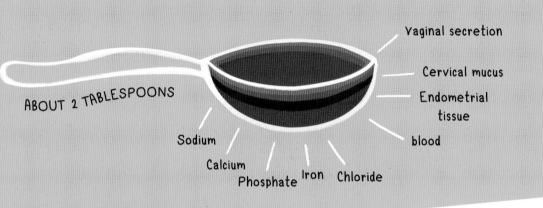

ABOUT 2 TABLESPOONS

Vaginal secretion

Cervical mucus

Endometrial tissue

blood

Sodium

Calcium

Phosphate

Iron

Chloride

Menstrual blood can be different colors or textures. It can be darker red, a bit brown, pinkish, or bright red. It can be thick or thin, and flow more quickly or more slowly. Some people have light spots of blood or a watery pink liquid just before their period starts.

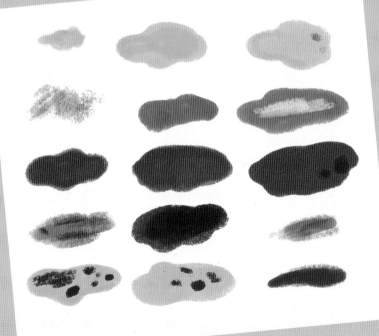

Will I run out of blood?

Some people are scared to see a lot of blood at once. It's because our brains have evolved to protect us, and bleeding often means we have been hurt. But menstrual blood isn't linked to injury—it's the lining that the uterus makes to create a safe, cozy place for a fertilized egg. It helps to remember that when you see your period blood!

Clots

Sometimes your menstrual blood can clot, especially if you have a heavy day or a heavy cycle. Clots are thicker clumps and are often about the size of your fingertip. There may be one or more mixed in with the rest of your period blood. They look a bit like jam or jelly that is dark red or black. If you squish a clot in some toilet paper, though, it will be red. That's because it's made of blood cells that thickened very quickly, and it looks dark because there are so many of them. It may be surprising to see clots if you get them, but they are usually nothing to worry about.

My story

At first, I thought that clots looked like bits of liver, and I was convinced my liver was falling out of my uterus! (Don't worry. This is impossible and can not happen.) Then I realized clots were pretty cool looking!

what do periods feel like?

I'm sure it won't surprise you to hear that periods feel different for different people at different times. I will try to describe it anyway, because talking about how periods feel and comparing notes is a great way to find out what other people experience, and also to find solutions if you or a friend finds periods very uncomfortable.

Here it comes!

You can't hold in a period—it just comes out. This means that you don't get an "I gotta go!" feeling like you may get when you have to pee or poop. Sometimes you can't feel periods at all. You just notice blood in your underwear or on your toilet paper or in the toilet bowl. Menstrual blood often comes out so slowly and in such small amounts at a time that you really don't notice it.

But then there are other times when you really *can* feel it. It often happens if you have a heavy flow day or got your period just after you went to bed. When you wake up in the morning and move to get out of bed, or even if you're just standing up from a chair after sitting for a long time, you can sometimes feel this weird, heavy sensation in your vulva. I always make my friends laugh by calling it the "flobbalobba" feeling. It really does feel as if a lot of gloppy stuff is coming out of your vagina at once, and if you go to the bathroom, you can usually see that it has. But it doesn't hurt, and I've always thought it was kind of funny.

FLOBBALOBBA

Other changes

Did you know that your cycle can cause changes in other parts of your body? Sometimes after ovulation you may feel what doctors usually call "breast tenderness." Your chest might feel full and heavy, or a bit sore. These sensations are caused by hormone changes and are usually a sign that you're at a new phase in your cycle. You might also find that you get pimples or that your skin becomes more oily or dry at a particular point in your cycle. You'll probably notice that these always happen at the same times. Knowing what's normal for you can help you recognize where you are in your cycle or remind you to stick to your skincare routine.

37

Cramping your style

Sometimes having your period can hurt, and you get cramps. They are caused by the muscles of your uterus pushing out the menstrual blood. That means a squeezy, tense feeling just below your belly button and under your bladder.

Since muscles and nerves that move your uterus are near so many other organs, the feeling can make your vulva, thighs, or lower back feel achy too. This also means you may have indigestion or need to do a very large poop, because the hormones that start your period can also affect your bowels. Exercise, dancing, or massage can really help cramps feel better. So can heat, but make sure you are using a hot water bottle or heat pad safely. Orgasms help too—it's like having a massage from the inside!

Did you know that you might feel crampy at other times of your menstrual cycle too? Sometimes, some people can feel a little twinge in their ovary when they ovulate, like a tiny pinch on one side or the other. This is called *mittelschmerz*, which just means "pain in your middle" in German.

Emotional changes

Just before your period starts, you may feel extra sad, tired, nervous, or excitable. Having to keep going as usual while feeling this way may cause you to act grumpy or lose your temper. This is known as PMS or pre-menstrual syndrome.

A good way to manage it is to notice when your period is due and plan some good self-care. Reminding yourself that you may be feeling extra sensitive can help you manage your emotions. In fact, knowing what happens to you during your cycle is a big part of managing it. Keep a diary over the course of several periods so that you know what happens to you at each point of the cycle. If something or someone is really bothering you though, don't blame your period—be proactive and try to solve that problem or tell someone how you feel!

My story

It's really common to feel constipated or have a really big poop just before or at the start of your cycle, but I didn't know that at first, and I thought it was just me! When I finally mentioned it to my friends I discovered they got it too! Now we call it "the period poop," which makes us laugh.

Charting your cycle

Now that we've talked about the different stages of the menstrual cycle, you may be able to recognize which phase you're in. Part of managing your period (and a very big step toward owning it!) is charting your menstrual cycle. This means keeping track of your period and other details of your whole cycle in a chart or graph.

There are a lot of fun, creative ways to do this. You can design a cycle chart by hand, using a pen and a ruler or compass. Or you could do it on a computer, using a table or a spreadsheet. You can decorate it with stickers, collages, or your own illustrations, and use lots of different colors. It can be something you leave on a shelf, carry with you, or display on your wall as a giant poster!

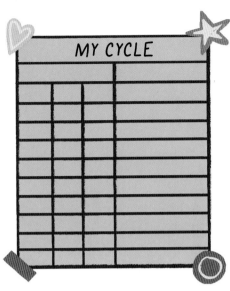

MY CYCLE

You might want to make columns and have one big chart for all the cycles in a year, or draw circles with wedges to have a new chart for each cycle. Here is the most useful information to show:

· **the start date**
(when you get your period)

· **the duration**
(the number of days your period lasts)

· **the length of cycle in days**
(this is the time from the start of one period to the start of the next one)

It's also worth having a box or separate section each month to log changes in your body, stressful events, happy events, travel, and any illnesses or injuries. All of these things can impact your cycle length or be a sign of changes in your hormones. You could also add a page or a section for the end of each year. It's an opportunity for you look back and sum up your average data and how you felt about your period that year.

My story

I used to just put a small dot in my homework planner, but I could barely find the dates again later. Finally, I made my own cycle chart zine and designed it to be used for 10 years. Then I could look back and notice how my period had changed over the years. I could also use it to see if any life events changed my cycle. I got much more comfortable with my period once I started writing down the details.

ADVENTURES IN MENSTRUATING!

CHELLA QUINT

Keep it simple

If you don't want to create a chart, you can also use a regular diary or calendar. A calendar design makes it easier to track your whole menstrual cycle and gives you space to log signs of ovulation and signs of PMS. Just remember not to throw it out at the end of the year—or you can copy your data and keep it somewhere safe.

This may sound like a lot to do, or like it's hard to remember, but it is actually pretty fun and it's a really healthy habit to have! It will also be really helpful if your doctor ever asks you whether you have regular periods. Some adults use their chart when they start thinking about their fertility.

With 12 months in a year, you might be expecting 12 cycles per year too. The reality is, you could have anywhere from 11 to 16 full cycles, depending on how long your cycle is. The dates don't exactly line up once per month.

42

Using an app

There are several different phone apps that can help you track your cycle. They let you keep track of information easily and learn interesting stats about your cycle more quickly than you could add them up yourself. There are now some apps that have been designed to be safer for use by young people, but only download and use one if you have permission from your adult.

Apps can be really useful, but they do have a few downsides. A lot of them were released by companies who sell menstrual products, and the apps are a way for them to advertise to new customers. Other apps sell your data to companies who want to learn more about how to advertise to you. It's more like *they* want to own your period!

If you decide to use an app now or in the future, choose an app that is:

✓ open about what it does with your data

✓ recommended by menstruation experts

✓ designed specifically for young people or has privacy and safety in mind

✓ inclusive and easy to navigate, with lots of colors and tracking options

Avoid apps that are:

✗ sponsored by a particular menstrual product or company

✗ secretive about what they do with your personal information

✗ designed for adults only

✗ all about wanting you to post pictures or speak to other members using social media

✗ full of stereotypes, like assuming someone's gender or their favorite colors

All about discharge

You've already learned about the menstrual blood that comes out during your period, but your cycle involves other fluids too. You may see them in your underwear or on your fingers or toilet paper and wonder what they are. They are forms of discharge—the fluids and substances produced by your reproductive system.

Healthy discharge

There are different types of regular discharge. Although they all look pretty similar, they come from different parts of the body, at different times, for different purposes. For example, the glands near the entrance to the vagina and urethra produce fluid to lubricate them and keep them clean and comfortable.

Sometimes your glands produce another fluid that lubricates the walls of the vagina, to make them smooth and slippery. This happens when you are feeling attractive, excited, or aroused.

There is mucus on your cervix too, and it changes throughout each cycle. Right before ovulation it looks like raw egg white or clear slime, and is very stretchy. It acts as a little ladder to help sperm reach an egg to be fertilized.

Changing hormones may make you sweat more as you go through puberty, including from the sweat glands around your vulva and anus. Your underwear may feel sweaty after a lot of activity or after sitting for a long time in a warm place.

Also, you may notice that the middle part of your underwear eventually fades or looks bleached over time. This is totally normal. Since vaginal fluid is naturally a bit acidic, it is common for healthy discharge to fade the gusset. Nothing is wrong with you... or your underwear!

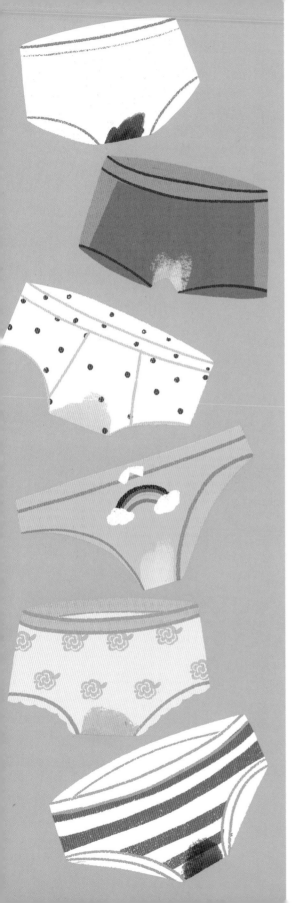

Unhealthy discharge

Your body is always working to maintain a healthy balance of the different types of bacteria that live inside you. Unhealthy discharge can sometimes mean an infection has been caused by a mismatch in the numbers of different types of bacteria.

Yeast infections are a common issue. They happen when the balance of bacteria types in your vagina gets disturbed. This can sometimes be caused by using soap inside your vulva or wearing tight underwear. Yeast infections itch and can make you sore, and they can produce a thicker discharge that looks a bit like cottage cheese. Bacterial vaginosis is another type of bacterial imbalance. It can produce gray, watery discharge that sometimes smells.

Sexually transmitted infections

Often called STIs, these are infections that can be passed on during sex. They may have symptoms that include a different smell, color, or texture to your discharge, as well as pain, bleeding, or itching. If you plan to be sexually active, you can ask for advice from your doctor or health clinic. Most STIs are treatable, and can be prevented by practicing safer sex.

when periods are a pain

Just like your blood pressure or heart rate, menstruation is part of your overall health. If you notice something unusual about your periods, it could be a sign of a medical condition. Some symptoms are very common, while others are much rarer. If you think anything is wrong or painful, even if it's not on the list, ask a doctor for help.

Where's my period?

Some people show signs of puberty before age 9, and others experience menopause during years that would usually be fertile. For most people though, if your cycle length becomes irregular or your periods stop for a few months there could be many reasons. They include stress, illness, trauma, hormonal conditions, big changes to your diet and exercise, and—if you're sexually active—pregnancy.

External pain

You may feel pain in your vulva or vagina. It could be a tight feeling, itchiness, swelling, or a burning sensation when you pee. These symptoms may be a sign of infection or injury, and a doctor should be able to find out the cause.

Internal pain

If you have painful menstrual cramps that make you feel sick or faint, or any sharp pains, or a dull ache in your pelvis or lower back in between your periods, you should ask a doctor about it.

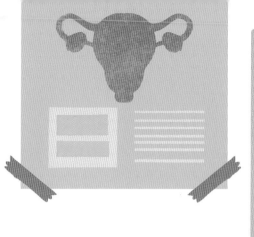

Something important to know about...

Genital cutting (sometimes called FGC) is one name for several types of surgery which may change the shape and sensations in the vulva. It is, or was, a traditional practice in some communities, but this procedure is now illegal in many places. Some cutting scars can cause pain or numbness and may change how periods flow from the vagina. If this affects you or someone you know, your doctor can make a referral to a specialist for expert help.

What's the problem?

Other medical conditions with some of these symptoms can be harder to diagnose, such as endometriosis and polycystic ovary syndrome (PCOS). There is also premenstrual dysphoric disorder (PMDD) where mental health can get low, but only at a certain time each cycle. These conditions are not that common, but if you're worried, don't be afraid to ask your doctor about them by name.

Keeping it in perspective

It is very rare for young people to experience most of the types of cancer that affect the reproductive system, but it is worth knowing how to ask about them in the future. Some people find it hard to talk about both cancer *and* periods, but don't let that stop you seeking help. Other than the symptoms already mentioned, bleeding between periods is one issue you should *always* see a doctor about.

Asking for help

Menstruation is a normal part of life. It's pretty typical to have a slight mood change, moderate cramping for a day or two, or a couple of days of heavier bleeding, followed by lighter days. However, other symptoms are not usual, and you don't have to put up with them. Menstrual problems can sometimes be a sign that something else is wrong, so you should always talk to a parent or doctor if you notice some symptoms.

Thinking that you might be getting ill can be worrying. This is especially true if you don't know exactly what's wrong, but just feel like *something* isn't right. Some illnesses and other problems related to menstruation are easy to treat, but hard to identify. Sometimes people—even parents and doctors—don't feel comfortable talking about periods. And not enough is known about some problems, because they haven't been thoroughly researched yet. But none of these are good enough reasons for you to suffer! You deserve to feel well.

Getting started

You may feel nervous about sharing a period worry with a trusted adult, or even comparing notes with a friend. Here are some conversation starters that might come in handy. You could even get together with a close friend or relative and practice using them.

Have you ever noticed that your period is...

I am worried that something is wrong with my periods because...

I have noticed that my cycle is irregular and I'm not sure why it has changed.

I get a lot of pain each month at the same time in my cycle. How can I find out what is wrong?

My periods are so heavy I don't know how to manage it. Can we find out why?

I haven't started my periods and I think I should have. Can we look into this?

I have been having some issues with my period. Can we make an appointment with a doctor, please?

I know this may be uncomfortable for you to talk about, but I need help.

I always get really depressed, anxious, and angry right before my period and it's affecting my life. I want to find out what's wrong and how we can change things.

49

Maintaining good period health

Your periods can affect your appetite, your energy and your skin.
So just as it's important to have a plan for when things go wrong,
it's really helpful to know what kind of habits support healthy periods.

Exercise

Regular stretching or core strengthening routines are a great idea for anyone. During your period, they can really help ease cramps. Regular exercise is also great for energy levels, mood, sleep patterns and general fitness throughout your cycle. A sudden change in your exercise routine can change or stop your periods for several months.

A healthy diet

Just before your period is due, you may crave foods with more sugar, salt, complex carbs and fat. But large quantities of these types of food can make you feel sluggish and bloated, so make sure to have plenty of vegetables, fruit and water as well. Maintaining a healthy diet helps maintain a regular cycle. Just like with exercise, a sudden weight gain or loss can change or stop your periods.

Skin and hair

You may find your skin changing at different times in your cycle as your hormones change. You might break out, or find that your skin is oilier or drier than normal. It helps to match your skincare routine to suit these changes. Just don't use any kind of soap, wipes, or other cleansers inside your vulva or vagina—these can cause infections. You can clean your outer labia with body soap or shower gel, but the inside cleans itself!

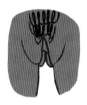

And, while we're on the topic of skin ... your vulva may be a different shade than the skin on your legs, face or other parts of your body. This is normal and healthy, and it is harmful to your body to try and change it. Look out for media messages that try to make people feel bad about this.

We all inherit different types and amounts of hair. Adults may choose to keep their pubic hair, trim it. or remove it entirely. Fashions change over time and by region, and people may or may not choose to follow these trends. You shouldn't feel pressured to do anything that you don't want to. Remember, we have pubic hair for a reason. It protects this delicate area and it helps prevent unwanted particles from entering the vagina.

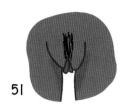

51

Your pelvic floor

A strong pelvic floor is important for holding in pee or poop, having better orgasms, and giving birth. As we age, these muscles can weaken, and certain things can put extra pressure on the pelvic floor. These include lots of trampolining, weighing more, being heavily pregnant, or giving birth. The best way to keep your pelvic floor muscles working well is to exercise them!

Most pelvic floor exercises involve squeezing the muscles. Have you ever tried to hold in pee? That's what squeezing your pelvic floor muscles feels like, though you shouldn't do these exercises while actually peeing.

You could try squeezing to lift up your vagina and perineum, then holding your muscles in the up position for 10 seconds, then slowly releasing. (This lifting is all on the inside—the outside of your body shouldn't move.) Or you could try ten quick squeezes. Repeat these exercises a few times in a row three times a day—start lying down, then do them sitting up, then standing. After a few months, your muscles will get stronger.

base of spine

uterus

pelvic floor muscles

pubic bone

bladder

rectum

urethra   vagina   anus

52

Look after your cervix

Your cervix can develop a particular kind of cancer caused by a virus called HPV (human papilloma virus). It can be prevented by having a vaccine before you become sexually active, and you can ask about it at your next check-up. It can also be successfully treated after that if the cervix is regularly checked by having a Pap smear. In a Pap smear, a doctor or nurse will insert a long brush into your vagina to collect cells from the cervix. The cells are tested in a lab to check for HPV and to look for changes that might lead to cancer.

cervical smear brush

Putting it all together

No one knows your body better than you do. When you feel comfortable looking at and feeling your body, and you know what's usual for you, it will make it easier to notice any changes—either good or bad. Think about what feels right and what looks right, and what kinds of products and routines work well for you. And don't forget that a good night's sleep helps *all* of your body's cycles! Make sure you take time to recharge and take steps to get back on track if your sleep habits change.

Menstrual supplies

There are lots of different menstrual products available. Young people sometimes just stick with the first product that was given to them, but there are so many different options to choose from—you can even make some of them yourself! Menstrual products can be either internal (worn inside the vagina) or external (worn outside the body). Each product is also either disposable (used once and then thrown away) or reusable (designed to be used again and again).

My story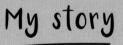

When I was young, no one told me about reusable products. When I finally found out and tried using them, I was so annoyed that I'd missed out! Instead of staying angry, I made up a dance: the Menstrual Product Mambo. I wanted a funny way to remind people that there was more out there than they might realize. There is so much variety now, and so many improvements to the different products, that I think it's worth celebrating!

Period underwear

"Period underwear" is the popular name for a specially designed type of underwear that includes extra layers for absorbing menstrual blood. These products are external and reusable. They look like ordinary underwear, but with a thicker gusset between the legs. The gusset's top layer lets the blood go through to a very absorbent middle layer, and a tightly woven bottom layer prevents blood from leaking through.

Using period underwear is incredibly easy. Some types are thicker and can be worn for up to 8 hours. That's good for a whole school day, or overnight. Thinner styles are better for the lighter days in your cycle, or combined with another product. You can buy period underwear online and in some stores. Most kinds can be washed with the rest of your clothes and should not go in the dryer, but always check the label.

Period underwear is comfortable, fashionable, and easy to use. On the downside, it can be a little bulky to carry a clean pair around, and if you want to change while you are out you'll need to store the used pair in a leakproof bag. Period underwear can also cost more money than regular underwear or disposable products. But they last several years, so will save you money in the long run. And they produce less waste!

Internal! External! Disposable! Reusable!

Dance along to your favorite mambo music!

55

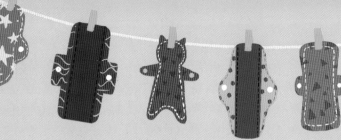

disposable

reusables

Menstrual pads

The other type of external product is a menstrual pad. Some pads are reusable and others are disposable, but they both work the same way: by covering the gusset of your underwear and absorbing menstrual blood.

Both types of menstrual pads have similar layers as period underwear. They come in different sizes and thicknesses to match your size, your flow, and even your style of underwear. Thin ones are called liners and go in your underwear or between your labia. Thick ones and night-time ones are often wider at the back to absorb more blood when lying down.

The two types of pads do have some differences. Disposable pads are often made from substances including plastic, which is not good for the environment. Reusable pads are made of fabric. Disposable pads are cheaper and more available to buy than a reusable one, but they can only be used once. Reusable pads last several years, so they work out cheaper over time. You can even make your own using online patterns! Each product is made of materials that may feel comfortable or uncomfortable to different people. Choose what feels right for your body.

External products and water

Period underwear and menstrual pads are external products, so they are not designed to use while swimming. Once the blood comes out of your body, it can't be absorbed by something that is already soaked! So even if you prefer to use external products, it may help to learn to use internal ones sometimes. Swimming can make cramps feel better!

Using pads

Disposable pads usually have an adhesive strip on the underside of the pad that sticks to your underwear to keep it in place. Many designs of disposable pad also have "wings" that help stop blood from leaking down the side of your underwear if the pad does move. It helps to stick the middle of the pad to your underwear first, before removing the backing that covers the wings and sticking them down. Some people bleed more toward the front, middle, or back, so you can position the middle of the pad wherever your heaviest flow is.

Reusable pads don't use adhesive because they are designed to be washed and worn again, but an adhesive strip would only be sticky enough to work once. Instead, cloth pads use snaps or hook and loop, and a few designs are folded.

Internal products

There are two types of internal products: ones that collect blood and ones that absorb it. They are useful for when you are swimming or doing any water-based activities because the blood is caught or absorbed before it can leave your body.

Menstrual cups

A menstrual cup is a reusable product that collects blood. It goes inside your vagina and forms a natural seal with your muscles that's a bit like a weak suction cup. The underside has a little stalk or ring that you use to pull it out. A menstrual cup needs to be emptied regularly throughout your period. You might empty it several times throughout the day, but on a light day you can leave it in for about 6 to 8 hours.

How to use a cup

With clean hands, pinch the cup in on itself or fold the top to make it narrower, then push it into your vagina. As you gently let it go, give it a little wiggle so that it opens up, and then check that it's comfy. To take it out, sit on or stand over the toilet, hold the stem or ring, put one finger up the side of the cup and push in a little bit to break the seal. Then you can either relax your muscles or push down (almost like you are going to poop), gently lower the cup, and tip it out over the toilet. Rinse the cup and put it back in, then wash your hands. It might sound complicated, but after a few tries it gets much easier!

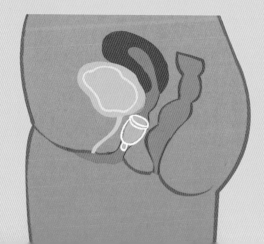

58

Choosing and caring for your cup

There are many different cups available, aimed at different ages of users with different levels of pelvic floor strength. You may need to try more than one kind to find out which type works best for you. Whatever the style, check that it is made of medical grade silicone. This reduces the risk of infection. If a cup is a bright color, check that the dye that was used is safe for products worn inside the body. There may not always be a sink handy to rinse the cup when you empty it, but make sure to clean it every night. At the end of your period, sterilize your cup by boiling it in a pan of boiling water or using sterilizing tablets. Then rinse it well, let it air dry, and store it in a breathable case. Always follow the instructions that come with your cup.

Why use a cup?
Menstrual cups are reusable and easy to carry around when you are expecting your period. They can be more expensive to buy but they are better for the planet than disposable products. And you can wear them when you go swimming or to the beach!

Tampons

Tampons are also inserted into the vagina, where they absorb blood rather than collecting it. Some tampons have an applicator, which is a little tube that helps push the tampon high into your vagina (a bit like a rocket booster!). Other tampons have no applicator, so you push them in with your finger. Both types are disposable—you throw them away once they are used (*don't* flush them!).

Which type should I choose?

There are many different designs of tampons, and you may need to try a few to find out which you prefer. Some people prefer non-applicator tampons because they are smaller and easier to carry around. They also have less packaging, so they are less wasteful. Other people prefer applicator tampons, especially if their fingers aren't very long.

Inserting a tampon

If you're using a non-applicator tampon, unwrap it with clean hands and unravel the string. Some brands of tampon let you use the string to widen out the base so you have a place to put your finger. Put the tip of the tampon in your vaginal opening and push it up as high as you can, so it's close to your cervix. (The diagram below shows the route the tampon will take, and you can try it first with just your finger.) Once the tampon is in place, wash your hands.

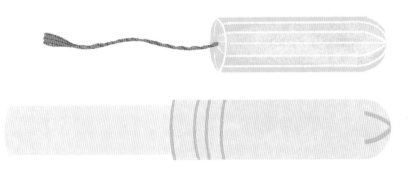

Applicator tampons have two pieces of tube that work like a telescope. You insert the tube into your vagina with the tampon at the top. You can take as much time as you want positioning the applicator, then you push the bottom bit up so the two parts fully overlap. This should push the tampon out of the top of the tube and into the upper part of your vagina. Remove the applicator and throw it away.

For either type of tampon, the string will be left hanging out of your vulva, so that you can pull the tampon out again. With some tampons, the string is a loop so that it's easier to grasp. If the tampon is bumping into your cervix, pull it a little bit lower. If it is still at your vaginal opening, you need to push it up more. If it hurts or feels uncomfortable, take it out and try again with a new tampon.

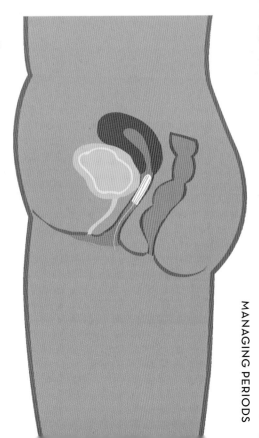

61

When to change?

A tampon should be changed every 4 to 6 hours, or sooner if it's full. The heavier your flow, the more quickly it will get full. Once it is full, blood can sometimes flow down the string or leak into your underwear. Tampons come in different absorbencies. Check the labels and have a few different absorbencies handy, and use the ones that are most suitable for each stage of your period. You should always use the lowest absorbency you need, and should change it regularly depending on your flow.

Staying safe

Tampons are made up of small fibers that may cause irritation. There is another concern though, a rare but serious condition called toxic shock syndrome (TSS), which has been linked to tampon use. Tampons carry extra oxygen into the vagina, which may cause bacteria to grow. This might make your body's immune system overreact trying to fight it, and though it often feels like the flu it can develop into something more dangerous. TSS is very unlikely, but get medical help right away if you develop aches, a fever, a rash, dizziness, or confusion while using tampons. Tampon packaging is required to mention TSS to help keep people safe.

You can reduce the risk of TSS. Do not use a higher absorbency of tampon than you need, remember to change your tampon, and don't forget to take it out on the last day of your period. There have been cases reported of a menstrual cup causing TSS, but this is extremely rare. To use your cup safely, make sure it is completely sterilized between cycles and stored in a cool dry place out of direct sunlight.

You may have heard of people using sea sponges as natural tampons, but sponges should not be used as menstrual products. Sea sponges are reef organisms that feed on tiny creatures and plant life, and some of this can remain even after the pieces of sponge are trimmed and washed. This organic matter may cause infections. Sponges also carry the same risk of TSS as tampons.

Saving the planet

Menstrual products are designed for a very sensitive part of the body, so many people want to know exactly what they are made of. Because of concerns about TSS and the chemicals used to make plastics, people started becoming more aware of how menstrual products are made. At the same time, they wanted to reduce waste by avoiding single-use products and extra packaging. These changes in attitude have led to a lot more choice when it comes to menstrual products... as you're about to discover!

Sustainability

Managing menstruation involves a lot of choices. You can choose based on how comfortable or practical a product is, or how much it costs. A lot of people also choose based on how much impact the products have on the environment. Caring about sustainability is everyone's responsibility, but your choices can inspire people around you to be more sustainable too! If you can't choose the most sustainable options now, you can ask for help finding or paying for them, and make plans to switch in the future.

Researchers estimate that an average person might use about 11,000 disposable pads and tampons in their lifetime. That's a lot! What's worse, these products (along with their applicators and packaging) could end up in landfills or, if accidentally flushed, as pollution in rivers or oceans, or along coastlines.

Most menstrual products and their packaging include plastic that gets thrown away after just one use. Many countries have made laws to reduce the use of some single-use plastics, but not of disposable menstrual products. The laws may change in the future, but in the meantime, you can make choices that help protect the environment.

Sustainability checklist

When choosing menstrual products, ask yourself:
• What are they made of?
• How far away are they made?
• What is the packaging made of?
• Does it list the ingredients?
• If the products are reusable, have they come from very far away or are they made nearby?
• Have you been able to buy them locally?
• Do the makers have other ethical policies, such as fair pay for their workers?
• If the company is owned by a big corporation, what are their policies for protecting the environment and human rights?

Take action!

Sustainability isn't just about what you buy. Why not design an eye-catching bathroom sign, reminding people not to flush menstrual products? Or research different cloth pad designs and try sewing your own! (You can be even more eco-friendly by upcycling some of your favorite clothes to use for fabric as they wear out.) You could also try different types of products over a few cycles and keep a comparison diary. Figure out how much you've spent, the number of times you've changed your product, and the amount of products, plastic, and packaging you've thrown away. Share your results with your friends and compare notes.

DON'T FLUSH

Worrying about stains and odor

Sometimes one of the first signs that you have started your period is a stain in your underwear. Other times you don't notice until the blood leaks through onto something else, like your clothing or the chair you were sitting on.

Removing stains

Blood can stain fabric, but it's easy to get out with a little bit of effort. As soon as possible, pre-treat it with stain remover and a cold-water soak. Scrub it and immediately wash it the way you would normally wash clothes, sheets, or bath towels.

Stain removers can sometimes take some color out of clothing, so you may want to try a tiny bit of laundry soap, dishwashing liquid, or hand soap instead. If this is a job only one person in your family does, you can do the soaking and scrubbing, offer to help, or just have a very open talk with them and ask if they will do it.

My story

At first, I used to leave any period stains that got on my underwear until the end of my period because I was embarrassed. When my mom found out, I had a lot of extra scrubbing—and explaining—to do! To help others get over their embarrassment, I did an art project that turned the stain itself into a comedy fashion accessory that I named STAINS™. I wanted to "rebrand" a period stain so it was trendy. I felt much better, and so did lots of other people!

What about smells?

When menstrual blood is inside your body, and even while it's inside your underwear or pad for a few hours, it doesn't really smell. Sometimes kids say "you smell" as an insult, but this is very rarely true, so don't assume they can smell you. (And you definitely don't need scented menstrual products—they include ingredients that can irritate your vulva.) What is true, though, is that menstrual blood can smell pretty bad if it's left out for a long time. It's best to throw disposables away in a trash can with a lid, and empty it within a couple of days.

What's the big deal about stains?

Stains happen, no matter what product you use. A lot of messages about leaks—from advertising, packaging, and other people—claim that they're weird or horrible. But actually, they're more of an inconvenience. After all, sports can make you sweat or leave your sneakers a bit stinky. That's just another example of bodies and bodily functions meaning that we need to look after what we wear. Stains shouldn't be something we worry about that much, but people still do. As for why that is… you'll find out in the next chapter!

PERIOD POSITIVITY

When I first learned about periods, everything I heard was negative, and adults seemed embarrassed about the topic. That made me a little bit scared to talk about it. This was because periods are a taboo. A taboo is something that a community tries to avoid doing, showing, or being around. Periods can also be seen as a stigma: something people don't discuss because it is considered bad, or bad luck.

Back then, I thought those negative feelings were how it had to be. But as I started to think about it more, I realized that the negative feelings hadn't started with me. I didn't have to hold onto them! Talking out loud about periods helped me challenge negativity. I did lots of activities and art and writing projects that helped me feel better, and I started sharing what I was doing with other people.

I called these actions being "period positive." This means understanding menstrual cycles, talking out loud instead of whispering, not being afraid to ask questions, and not worrying too much about leaking or stains. Now the idea of period positivity is spreading—like a big period stain!

Menstrual shame

Periods bring up all kinds of emotions —both for people who have them and people who don't. Taboos can make you feel ashamed if you are "caught" doing or talking about the taboo thing. This can also lead to a feeling that some people are avoiding you or avoiding the topic in lots of little ways that can make you feel uncomfortable or in trouble—even if you're not.

Shame is a feeling that makes you think you're bad if you're doing something considered embarrassing or wrong. You might feel shame if you hurt someone's feelings or were unkind, and that can feel awful. Feeling shame about periods can really lower your self-esteem and trick you into feeling like you or your body is bad or wrong. And that's not fair!

My story

When I was nearly 13, I was at a slumber party when I leaked menstrual blood onto my nightgown, and the other girls teased me for letting it happen. I was so embarrassed I wanted to hide. Now I want to help people worry less about leaks and more about breaking down the stigma around leaking.

70

The past...

Throughout history, a few communities around the world have actually thought periods were good or special and several other cultures have gone back and forth on it. Unfortunately, most communities held negative beliefs, and many still do. For a long time, a lot of people haven't felt they had much ownership of their periods because of these unspoken (and sometimes spoken!) rules about them.

... And the present!

Most of these rules aren't around anymore, but shame is still a very strong emotion. Although you shouldn't be ashamed of your natural bodily functions, it's hard to stop feeling this way while the attitudes are still around. When those attitudes go away, though, the people who have periods will start to feel less embarrassed by them, and will feel empowered about other things too.

The good news is that attitudes are starting to change. People everywhere are starting to agree that menstruation is simply a natural part of how a healthy body works—a good thing we should talk openly about and help with when there's a problem, whatever our gender. It has taken a long time to change this attitude, and it's happening slowly. To speed up the pace so we can feel better right now, let's look at how these attitudes have ended up affecting us for so long.

SHAME

Busting myths and slaying superstitions

Taboos often start as old ideas that get out of control, but as we learn more, we pay less attention to those messages. When something has as many negative messages around it as periods, though, it can be hard to figure out where they came from, or if they're true. Sometimes there is misinformation out there. What do you do if you hear something about periods and it doesn't seem accurate? What attitudes have kept these beliefs going for so long, even when so many things are changing for the better? Let's break down some myths and superstitions into categories so we can take a closer look.

"The way menstruating bodies work is a total mystery!"

Well, if you've read the first half of this book, you know that's not true. But it used to be! Doctors in ancient Greece believed that the uterus could float around the body and make you sick or affect your mental health. This idea was still floating around (ha!) in the UK in Victorian times, because some doctors who read it in ancient books believed it.

In fact, the uterus doesn't float around the body like a hot air balloon. It's attached by ligaments inside your pelvis, and its position does not make us ill. We now know a lot about menstruation, but because of some of the other myths and fears people have had, we don't know as much as we should—at least, not yet. More research into menstrual health is being funded and carried out every day, and it's long overdue.

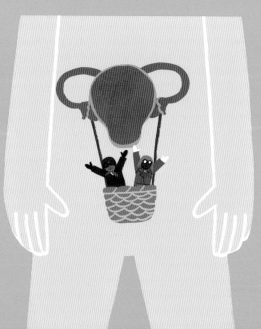

"Periods synchronize with the moon ... and with other periods!"

When something can't be explained, people make up stories and share their own explanations. Periods being linked to the moon is a very popular story across many cultures past and present, and it's a lovely idea, but I'm sorry to say that there is no scientific evidence that the moon controls menstrual cycles. For some people the moon's cycle and the menstrual cycle may be the same length, but that's where the similarity ends.

It's also not true that people who live together always get their period on the same day as each other. Lots of scientific research was done over long periods of time with people who lived together, and there was no evidence it really happens. Even though friends or family members may notice it when they do get their period at a similar time, it's just a coincidence, and often something fun to talk about.

73

"Menstrual blood is dirty and dangerous!"

Some people say that menstrual blood will attract animals, or that it will bring bad luck or keep you from doing things. But will it really? Sharks won't attack someone at the beach just because they have their period. They're actually repelled by menstrual blood! There have been no reported cases of bears attacking campsites just because menstrual products were around, although it's important to take your litter with you. (This is not to say that animal encounters don't ever happen. But if they do, it won't be because of your period.)

Seeing blood on the outside of your body can stir up an instinct in the animal bit of your brain that makes you think you're injured or in danger. There is a theory that some ancient people may have thought that periods were a sign of serious illness or a warning of bad times.

But in fact, periods are a sign that your body is well. They're not something terrible that happens to you—they're something amazing your body can do! It's important to remember that people in the past didn't know how the body worked. They also had different interpretations of clean and dirty, good and bad, and right and wrong. In many communities, menstruating people were not allowed to do certain activities—such as cooking, farming, or harvesting food—because menstrual blood was considered so powerful that it could poison or spoil food. Even though we now know that periods are healthy, echoes of these negative messages that uphold the old myths still exist.

Just as people were advised not to cook certain foods on their periods, they were also advised not to shower, swim in cold water (or at all!), or do any exercise. In several faiths, some religious activities were forbidden if you had your period. It was also considered taboo to have sex during your period. But medical, religious, and sexual health advice is changing—periods are no longer a barrier to participating in community life. And remember, orgasms make cramps feel better! Your cycle may affect your sports training routine, and heavy periods or cramps can disrupt your day, but otherwise no one can stop you from doing anything just because you menstruate.

"You shouldn't talk about menstruation out loud."

Many people seem to think that if you absolutely have to talk about menstruation, you should call it something else, and only talk in whispers. When they talk about a topic they feel is stigmatized, people often call it by a euphemism. A euphemism is a word or phrase people use in place of a more uncomfortable or sensitive one. Euphemisms are often used to describe menstruation. Some people call it a visitor or a friend, or Aunt Flo (like "flow" ... get it?). Other people joke about the color of their underwear, and some people just use a secret code like "I got it." Some euphemisms reinforce those old taboos about periods being dirty or dangerous—such as calling a period something like "the curse." Even the word "period" is a euphemism! It's short for "menstrual period."

There is a lot of truth to the belief that naming something gives it power. Calling menstruation by its proper name—menstruation—is empowering! Talking openly makes things less scary. It also helps teach others by setting a good example.

My story

When my grandma was a teenager she would say, "I can't go swimming because I have my friend." And the other kids knew what she meant! When she told me this I couldn't believe it. But I liked the idea of her period being her friend, even if she was just saying what others did, to avoid the stigma.

"You should keep it a secret that you have your period."

Imagine you were not doing an activity because you were expected to avoid it during your period, but you couldn't tell anyone that was the reason. It may seem silly, but that's the situation a lot of people found themselves in all the time a generation or two ago, and some still do.

Because people felt they couldn't talk about periods, they also believed that no one should see them. People were expected to hide their menstrual products—and their menstrual blood too! That's why ads for menstrual products often use blue liquid instead of red. But remember that menstrual blood and period leaks don't need to be hidden and having it happen shouldn't make anyone feel ashamed. Accidents happen, no matter what products you use. You don't need to hide the fact that you have periods or the way that you manage them.

Media messages: a timeline

You'd be surprised how many echoes of the old myths are still around. You find them in the way that menstrual products are advertised. These ads have only been around for 100 years, but they've been a huge influence on modern stigma and taboos.

Most people made their own pads out of cloth or wore a red petticoat to protect their clothing. Some catalogs advertised rubber aprons and baggy underwear for the same purpose. After World War I, bandage companies rebranded their bandage rolls as disposable menstrual products made from cotton-like wood pulp. Some early types included moss.

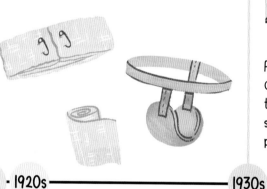

Ads for pads focused on the "horror" of leaks. Of course, the problem these products promised to fix still happens! But these worries were starting to catch on, along with the idea that pads could "save" you from leaking.

Pre 1920s - 1920s ————————— 1930s ——————

Ads pushed the idea that these "sanitary hygiene" products were healthier and easier to hide than homemade cloth ones. They tried to convince people that periods were dirty and embarrassing, implying that buying menstrual products would keep you from seeming poor or old-fashioned. Some brands worded their ads as though they came from doctors and nurses to be extra convincing.

78

Innovations like a belt to hold up your pad became popular, but because of World War II, the ads started using wartime words like "shield" and "protection." Whispering became a feature—connecting talking openly about periods with the life-or-death urgency of military secrets. These words and ideas stuck, even after the war.

The fashions changed, but the messages still focused on hygiene, secrecy, and leak prevention. The rise of tampons meant lots of ads promoted how useful they were for swimming. Pad and tampon companies started sending sales reps to visit schools with leaflets and free product samples, hoping to gain loyal customers.

More ads focused on teens, hoping they would start using a particular brand and remain loyal for life. Ads were designed to look similar to popular teenage magazines, with cartoons and captions. Teen characters talked about sports, "freshness," and new scented products that reinforced worries about odor. New pad shapes and adhesive backing became popular.

This brand helps me cope!

1940s — 1950s — 1960s — 1970s

Companies disguised boxes of menstrual products as fancy soaps or cute stationery, so no one would know what you were buying. There were also ads for "feminine hygiene wash" to keep you feeling "dainty" (hinting that periods made you smelly!). Some ads just showed someone in a ballgown alongside the pad's brand name, suggesting their products would save you from leaks or pad outlines ruining your fancy clothing.

PERIOD POSITIVITY

79

Blue liquid became very common in advertising, along with blue packaging. Gymnasts were shown in several commercials and print ads, continuing the sports theme. In the USA in 1985, the word "period" was used for the first time in a TV commercial, but product names and packaging still barely hinted at what was inside. Some tampons were recalled from stores or taken off store shelves because of links to toxic shock cases.

BLUE LIQUID

Advertising and school leaflets stayed the same, sharing messages of secrecy. Some slogans focused on empowerment but seemed patronizing, and others showed tampons in disguise again. Viral marketing, websites, and apps appeared that seemed educational but were created by menstrual products companies, ultimately pointing readers toward their products. There was still lots of blue liquid, but marketing, products, and packaging became plastic and very pink. Luckily, reusable products were becoming an alternative.

1980s	1990s	2000s

Ads in teen magazines portrayed periods as uncomfortable, with their products "saving" you from leaks. They claimed to "know how you feel," but were clear that periods and menstrual products were embarrassing (especially in front of anyone male!). Some advertising even encouraged you to hide tampons by pretending they were something else. Thin pads with wings became popular. Many schools still taught about periods using company leaflets and free samples in girl-only groups.

Because people started talking more openly about periods and questioning the messages about them, some companies' advertising finally changed. They started mocking themselves, using "activist" characters to challenge their old messages. Menstrual cups, cloth pads, and period underwear were becoming more popular, and they were promoted with funny and taboo-breaking ad campaigns. Advertising for reusables was often more honest—and got rid of the blue liquid! Finally, a disposables company also started using red liquid in ads.

2010s

The future!

It took a lot of determination from activists to make menstrual products and advertising safer, more sustainable, more ethical—and less taboo. People are starting to recognize the good in talking about periods, even if (*especially* if!) they make us feel bad. But a lot of people still worry about periods—and society often backs that up. So what happens next? Here are my wishes for the next decade:

• Governments change the law to make companies more accountable for their products and advertising techniques, and stop brands from influencing governments or schools.

• Schools get the funding to train teachers and other staff to improve menstruation education and include media literacy and sustainability.

• Companies and campaigners keep listening, and update their products and messages to be more useful, inclusive, and accurate.

• All people keep learning about menstruation and sharing that knowledge, whether they menstruate or not!

Being a period positive consumer

Despite some changes, many of today's menstrual product ads keep those old myths going. Are they hiding products, disguising packaging or using words like "whisper," "secret," or "discreet"? These are signs they are using shame to sell. Using words like "hygiene," "protection," and "sanitary," only referring to blood as "fluid" or "moisture," or making promises about leaks all imply that periods are dirty and blood is scary.

It is not okay to use shame and taboo to win over customers. No one can own how *you* feel about periods but *you*! So if you want to be a taboo-savvy consumer, here are some tips.

Start a media diary

Look out for menstrual messages in films, TV, ads, signs, news broadcasts, and online. Why are periods in the news? Is the way people represent them positive, negative, or neutral? What images are included? Who gets mentioned? It might be companies, activists, celebrities, politicians, doctors, teachers, students, parents, or researchers. All of these choices tell a story.

Compare advertising and packaging

Visit local stores, check packaging designs, and decide which ones are being honest. Look out for taboo warning words! Does the packaging give useful info about what's inside, how it works and what it's made of?

Comparison shop for reusables

When buying reusables, read reviews of the brands. See which ones have good reviews or great customer service. You can even compare prices and figure out how many times you'd need to use a reusable to match the cost of the disposables you'd be replacing.

Go with a buddy

Ask a friend or relative to look at menstrual products with you. It's great to have someone to bounce ideas off and see if you agree about some of the messages.

Ask for what you want

New products come out all the time—stay in the know so you don't miss a thing! If you live somewhere that offers free menstrual products to young people, or if a relative buys products for you, ask for what you want. You deserve a say about the products purchased on your behalf.

Invent your own menstrual product

Try designing your own menstrual product. You might even be able to find someone at school or a local college who will help you make a prototype! Design packaging and ads for your product that help break taboos. Use puns, be silly, and have fun!

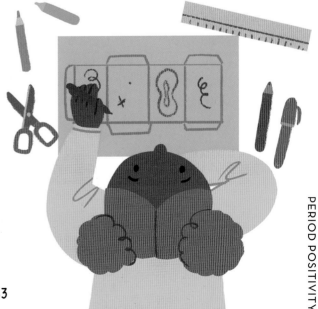

Talking about periods

How did you first learn about periods and puberty? Many people learn from friends and family, or by seeing films or advertising. Did the people you learned from seem confident and knowledgeable? And how comfortable do you feel talking about periods now? Here's a guide to starting the conversation and keeping it going.

Too much information?

Periods can be kept private, but they definitely should not be a secret, and no one should say otherwise. Sharing your knowledge and experiences can be empowering, but keeping your worries to yourself can make them feel much worse. The more you share, the more your comfort zone will expand.

Ssh!

How comfortable talking about periods are you?

I keep it to myself

close friend(s) and/or family

wider friends/family and community

Everyone!

Being inclusive

None of the information in this book is meant only for people who have periods. Everyone's experiences and identity shape their view of periods, and the more people know, the easier menstruation is to manage. If the people making laws and ads years ago knew what you know now, things would be a lot more period positive! So it's important for everyone to find ways to talk about periods. Not everyone likes periods and not everyone has them, but even if it gets uncomfortable, it's important to share and celebrate differences, not ignore them.

Reclaiming slang

Skip the euphemisms, but don't feel like you have to avoid NEWphemisms. That's the word I use for nicknaming your period, so that it feels like a friend, not an enemy. Just make sure you're not trying to hide what's happening from yourself or someone else. Also, menstruation puns are super fun. See if you can spot a few now. They come in *waves*. It's hard to ab*stain* from punning when I'm in full *flow*. Get it? Laughing about periods is awesome and puns are a very easy way to start. *Period.*

Use "menstruation" proudly

If you feel like menstruation is not your word, I'm here to tell you it is. It's multilingual, medical, useful, and clear – and it's not just for doctors or grown-ups. I've stopped saying "feminine hygiene" and "sanitary products" and instead I say "menstrual products," and I feel so much better. Naming things your body can do can help you feel confident and powerful. It can also help others learn healthy ways to think and talk about periods, whether they menstruate or not.

Navigating periods at school

You may be feeling more period positive, but others might not be feeling the same way as you—at least, not yet! How can you help build an environment that helps everyone to learn more about periods and manage them confidently, without being stopped by the issues that taboo and stigma can cause? Here are some steps you can take to help make your world more period positive.

Evaluate your school

How period positive is your school? Are you allowed to go to the restroom during class? Do your lessons include information on periods? Do all genders get lessons on menstruation together? Are your teachers trained and trusted when it comes to period talks? Do they teach about reusable products and sustainability? Do they avoid brand names or logos? Do they include all genders, abilities, and cultures?

Make a list of things your school (or club or team) can do better, and get expert advice to make those things happen. You could talk to your school about teaching more about reusable products or ask for menstruation to be a topic across a wider variety of subject areas, like learning to make packaging or pads in design and technology.

My story

I did this kind of evaluation once and noticed that all the leaflets and books about puberty showed illustrations of miserable-faced children, and used negative words like "coping" or "suffering" rather than "managing." I started asking for those things to be changed and I didn't stop, and now the words are even changed in England's national school curriculum guide.

Spread the word!

Ask if you can teach an activity to your class, team, or group. Plan a trivia quiz, teach the menstrual product mambo, or design a whole lesson for your class based on what you've learned. If it goes well, share it with others to teach in their classes or groups!

Try craftivism

When you combine crafts and activism, you get *craftivism*! If you can knit, bake, crochet, sew, illustrate, design, or build, you can be a craftivist! Crochet a uterus or make vulva cupcakes. Use beads and elastic cord to make a period bracelet, using different beads to represent different phases of your cycle. I like to debunk leakage fear by using that bright-red stain shape I designed to make pins, jewelry and stickers. You can too!

87

Share the Period Positive Pledge

I coined the term "period positive" in 2006 and it has spread all over the world like a great big friendly period stain. This guide will help you help others and make sure that when you work on breaking menstrual taboos, you're doing it in a fair, positive, and respectful way.

1 Say "menstrual products" instead of "feminine hygiene," "sanitary products," or "femcare." It's time to move on from phrases that make periods sound dirty or that we have to be sterotypically "feminine" to use them.

2 When you talk about periods, don't leave anyone out, because everyone deserves to learn.

3 Find out how to use sustainable menstrual products and aim to cut single-use plastics out of your menstruation management. Then tell people why you're doing that.

4 Remind yourself (and others too) of details about the whole menstrual timeline—from menarche to menopause.

5 Check that your home, school, and other locations have everything that someone who menstruates would need. If not, try to make changes.

6 Study the biology of reproductive health so that you understand how your body functions healthily, and can recognize when things are going wrong.

7 Fight for the rights of people whose menstruation causes extra worries because they are facing discrimination in another part of their lives.

8 Remember that education, training, and choice make it easier for people to manage menstruation.

9 Challenge companies who still use stereotypes, fear, or taboos in advertising for their products.

10 If you want to share something you've seen about periods, give credit to the person who created it.

11 If you find out something about periods that you want to share, make sure it comes from a trustworthy source.

12 When you see companies working with schools or charities, try to figure out why they are doing it. Is it mostly so they can advertise to you, or do they really want to listen and help people?

13 If a person makes a mistake when they're talking about periods, it's okay to correct them. But do it in private, so that you don't embarrass them.

14 Remember that lots of information about periods is still being discovered, and there is always more to learn.

15 Never feel ashamed or embarrassed about your body, puberty, or periods.

16 Question the messages you see in advertising, films, online, in books, on television, and in other media if they show periods in a negative way.

17 Be proud to use the word "menstruation" more often when discussing periods. Avoid whispering or using negative euphemisms or secret gestures to keep it hidden.

18 Compare notes with friends and relatives to figure out what is healthy for your body and see a doctor about any menstrual problems.

19 Remember that anyone of any age, race, gender, sexuality, ability, background, or culture can talk about menstruation. Make sure the people most affected have space to speak for themselves. If this is you, be proud and take up space!

20 Ask questions and be open and welcoming of new ways of looking at menstruation.

Own it!

This book is an owner's manual for your period. How much did you know before you started reading? Congratulations on taking the time to get to know it better! This may be the end of the book, but it's just the beginning of your relationship with menstruation. From now on, share what you know, and ask plenty of questions!

The more people know about periods, and the more they talk about them, the fewer menstrual taboos there will be, and that means that they won't be passed on any longer. You probably already know a lot of people who could learn from what you know now. Everything in this book is absolutely yours to share and there are a lot of fun ways to share it. You've got all this great menstrual knowledge—now it's your turn!

Don't forget the past

When I first started thinking about menstrual taboos many years ago, I interviewed my mom, my sister, my grandma, and my male best friend. You may want to interview a relative too! Not everyone will want to be interviewed, but you won't know unless you ask. Everyone has a period story, whether they menstruate or not. Remember – everybody once had a room that was a womb! Base your questions on the chapters in this book. Ask about how they learned, what they think of periods now, and what they recommend for the future. How will you save this interview? You could turn it into a comic or make a video.

Think about the future

Be ready for questions from younger friends and family members. Think about how you will explain periods to them. Try this: you can talk about the blood being like a pillow and blanket that the uterus makes to protect a new baby before it's born. And why does the uterus make the pillow and blanket out of blood? Because it can't go to the store! Blood is squishy and the body makes some every day, so it's a perfect comforter for the womb room.

Now it's your turn

We may never know all there is to know about periods, but we are learning all the time, and this is everything I know right now. I'm going to keep finding out more, and talking about it more, and I hope you will too. So learning how to be period positive doesn't end now—it starts now. And it's going to be great!

including everyone

cycle charting

asking questions

informed choice

talking out loud

wellbeing

Glossary

Adhesive A sticky backing that works like glue to hold something, such as sticking a pad to your underwear

Anus The opening in your bottom where poop comes out

Arousal An excited feeling, usually to do with wanting to feel good sexually

Bacteria Tiny living things that live and grow on other living things. Some are useful but others can cause illnesses

Cervix The lower part of the uterus that opens into the vagina. It is made of strong muscle tissue

Clitoris The sensitive organ that provides sexual pleasure and produces orgasms. It starts at the top of the vulva and continues under the skin

Clot A clump of thickened blood that has formed a jelly-like blob

Contraception Something that helps to prevent conception or pregnancy

Cramps Pain caused by a muscle contracting. Cramps during your period are caused by the uterus contracting to push out the uterine lining

Discharge Fluid produced in the cervix or vagina. Most types of discharge are healthy and normal, but some can indicate an infection

Disposable (also called **single-use**) Designed to be used once and then thrown away

Egg cell (also called an **ovum** or plural **ova**) A cell that, if fertilized by sperm, can implant into the wall of the uterus, leading to pregnancy

Endometrium The blood-filled tissue that lines the uterus

Estrogen The hormone that controls many parts of the menstrual cycle, including triggering an egg cell to mature

Euphemism A word or phrase someone uses to replace a word that makes them feel uncomfortable, or that they worry will make someone else uncomfortable

External menstrual product A product that is worn outside the body to absorb menstrual blood

Fertile Able to produce eggs and conceive babies

Follicle A small fluid-filled cavity in the ovary that contains a developing egg cell

Gland One of several organs that produce chemicals that are either released into the body or pass out of the body

Glans The rounded tip of the clitoris or penis

Gusset The fabric in the middle of a pair of underwear

Hormone One of the chemicals produced by the body that control various biological functions

HPV (short for **human papillomavirus**) A family of commonly transmitted viruses that can cause genital warts and some types of cancer

Internal menstrual product A product that is worn inside the vagina for collecting or absorbing menstrual blood

Labia The inner and outer folds of the vulva

Ligament A band of tough tissue that connects bones or supports muscles or organs

Lubrication A slippery substance that coats a surface to reduce friction and allow smooth movement

Media literacy The ability to identify the meaning of the messages contained in different types of media such as advertising or websites

Menarche (pronounced MEN-ar-kee) The time when someone has their very first period

Menopause The time in life when menstrual cycles end

Menstrual cup A silicone cup that is inserted into the vagina to collect menstrual blood

Menstrual pad A disposable or reusable product made of absorbent and moisture-wicking layers, worn inside the underwear to absorb menstrual blood

Mucus A slimy substance produced by body parts called mucous membranes, which is used for lubrication or protection

Organic Having to do with or coming from living things. It can also describe a product that is produced without using pesticides or other added chemicals

Organ A body part, such as the heart or skin, that performs a particular task

Orgasm A feeling that releases a lot of excitement and pleasure in the body

Ovary One of the pair of glands that produce, store, and mature egg cells

Oviduct (also called **Fallopian tube**) One of the tubes that carries an egg cell from the ovary to the uterus

Ovulation The release of an egg cell from the ovaries

Pelvic floor The muscles at the base of the pelvis that support organs such as the bladder, uterus, and colon

Pelvis The area of the body between the hips that contains the reproductive organs

Perineum The sensitive area between the vulva and the anus

Period underwear A reusable menstrual product designed with a cloth pad built into the gusset

Puberty The time at which young people's bodies change as they mature into young adults who are able to reproduce

Pubic hair The hair that can cover the pelvic area, thighs, and belly

Reproductive system The parts of the body involved in producing babies

Reusable Designed to last rather than be thrown away after a single use

Shame A feeling stronger than embarrassment that makes a person feel like they are bad or wrong, or that they will be judged for something about their personality, actions, or situation

Sperm A type of cell that is needed to fertilize an egg cell to start a pregnancy

Stereotype A widely-held but oversimplified and often inaccurate idea of a particular type of person or thing

Sterilize To make something free of bacteria, often by boiling or steaming

Stigma A belief that someone is bad or wrong because they did something that is thought to be shameful

Superstition A belief, sometimes held by many people, that is not based on fact

Surrogate A person who carries and gives birth to a baby for someone else

Sustainability A way of meeting our needs by managing or using resources in a way that protects them and doesn't use them up

Taboo An unspoken rule in a community or culture that something should not be done or should not be talked about

Tampon A disposable menstrual product made of absorbent cotton or other material that is inserted into the vagina to absorb menstrual blood

Tampon applicator A small, two-part tube that acts as a plunger to help push a tampon higher inside the vagina

Toxic shock syndrome (TSS) A rare but very serious bacterial infection that has been linked to tampon use

Urethra A tube that carries pee from the bladder out of the body

Uterus An organ where an embryo can develop into a fetus. It grows a lining to protect an egg cell each month, and the shedding of this lining is part of the menstrual cycle

Vaccine A substance given to people to protect them from a particular disease by boosting their immunity to it

Vagina The sensitive, muscular passage leading from the vulva to the uterus

Vulva The external parts of the reproductive system of someone who has periods, including the clitoris, labia, and vaginal opening

Zine (short for magazine and pronounced ZEEN) A handmade or self-printed booklet or magazine that you can give away, sell, or swap

Index

Resources

To find out more about how you or the adults you know can become more Period Positive, visit Chella's Period Positive website:

www.periodpositive.com

If you'd like to see some amazing vintage menstrual product ads for yourself, check out the Ad*Access Archive at Duke University (use the search term "feminine hygiene" and then browse by decade):

repository.duke.edu/dc/adaccess

For information on lots of aspects of menstruation and reproductive health, especially if you want to become a menstruation researcher yourself one day, visit the Society for Menstrual Cycle Research:

www.menstruationresearch.org

Love from Chella
and Giovana!